Almost Naked

ALSO BY HADLEY HURY

The Edge of the Gulf

It's Not the Heat

Almost Naked

Poems

Hadley Hury

David Robert Books

Published by David Robert Books
P.O. Box 541106
Cincinnati, OH 45254-1106

ISBN: 9781625492913

Poetry Editor: Kevin Walzer
Business Editor: Lori Jareo

Visit us on the web at www.davidrobertbooks.com

Acknowledgments

The following poems appeared first in these publications:

New Year's Eve	*Off the Coast*
Photos of Our New Hydrangeas	*Avatar Magazine*
With You	*Appalachian Heritage*
That Boy from The '50s	*Appalachian Heritage*
October Clean	*The James Dickey Review*
The Rate of Disappearance	*The James Dickey Review*
Almost Naked	*Forge Journal*
Reading Chekhov Again	*Forge Journal*
Boy on the Beach	*Forge Journal*
Call and Response	*Evening Street Review*
Gingko	*Brink Literary Magazine*
Hush	*Vox Poetica*
Old Friends	*Vox Poetica*
Screens	*Vox Poetica*
Following the Moon	*Vox Poetica*
Mourning Doves	*Meadowlands Review*
Palliation	*Chapter 16*
The Last Snow	*Belle Reve Journal*
Meeting the New Trees	*Belle Reve Journal*
I Would Be White Tulips	*Lost Coast Review*

for Marilyn

Table of Contents

Photos of Our New Hydrangeas

After I opened the attachments and saw the three small shrubs
you planted yesterday,
and immediately wrote back
to say how proud I am of your good hard work
and that I hope you remember to stretch today,
I wondered for a moment how lace-cap hydrangeas
can snuggle into the autumn soil
without me to tell them how
to tuck their roots
and bow their heads
and sleep.

How can it be that one of us
has planted new life in our garden
without the other there to help?

In all things we have always grown together—
and so I could feel for a moment the three bushes
mulched in their new bed,

huddled along the north foundation wall,

the quilt of grass faded by early freezes

neatly folded at their knees,

and a chill slithered up

from my feet beneath this desk

to my fingers on this keyboard,

and I feel the waiting for you—

this half-life separation—

as slowed and quiet breathing,

dormant flesh and bone.

Call and Response

I could not know what it was.
There was not even the evidence of clues
and their fellows had left the scene.

Yet they drew me and I looked
and looked again at the two Canada geese
far from the lake and their usual haunts
improbably perched and proud and rearing
one high on the roof corner of one outbuilding
and the other high on the corner of another
some fifty yards away opposed in what
seemed to be a loud insistent quarrel.

I watched from the windows and then went outside
and stood quite still until with lowering necks
they eyed me and cocked their heads in curiosity
and then returned to the business at hand.

I tried to work at my desk but for over an hour
the breach that ebbed and flowed was so foreign
yet familiar that it circulated in my skin

like a baby's cry or shouts in the street
or the earthquake silence that can crack the world
before the doctor speaks or the pulsing throb
of a voice that scratches from some distant room
like a wind-troubled twig on the window
through a long winter night.

At some point later I realized
the birds were gone.

So much of life is at a slight remove
overheard or dreamed or untranslatable
but the sounds fill us as wind does sails
and carry us to the brink of places
where we may alight not on an island
but on some floating bridge of recognition
and know it is enough to say
I heard I have come I am near.

Boy on the Beach

The boy on the beach
stared out
not knowing then
the sea might someday evoke
simultaneous thoughts of
nostalgia and fear
life and death
love and loss
the certainty of beauty
the precipice of the howling void
infinity and inconsequence.

Instead there was then
a kind of comfort
a vague promise or hope
that the crowdedness in his
head was behind him
not here on this wide expanse
looking out to an unknown horizon
but back there

behind him

around the dinner table

in the classroom

on the schoolyard

in novels and at the movies

all that urgency toward definition

from without and within.

Time sloshed idly

with the foam through his toes

and the desperate competing stories

evaporated in the dusk

impossibly absurd

in the face of such openness

such benign and

blank regard.

Almost Naked

We spend our first years
learning to dress ourselves,
as in, look who put his shoes on
all by himself, or
what a big girl,
all those buttons!

After we discovered
that we couldn't judge a book by its cover,
and that everyone didn't always
mean what they said,
and that we would never,
as we once wanted, be a character in a book,
we sacrificed our innocence before
it turned out to have been
no better than our ignorance.

We still try things on:
taking time to read more cookbooks,

learning to assemble electronic devices without

existential despair and hurled instruction manuals,

trying to love the moronic neighbor down the road

with his guns and hysterical dogs,

looking back to see

not a life of losses and discards

but a fond trail of furnishings outgrown.

It's not that we may not have

the occasional embarrassment

over things that we have done

(the unaccustomed earring still on

as we crawl into bed),

and the things we have left undone

(the barn door,

as we stroll into the cocktail party),

it's just that now

some new sort of credulity beckons,

like that first Christmas morning

after we *knew*,

and yet had to walk on anyway,

toward the tree,

across a now grotesquely foreshortened living room,
remembering the perfectly contained skin
of our footed pajamas just a year before,
the first taste of something we'd later call
metaphor rising bitter in our mouths.

We still have our
baffled need to trust,
but more and more, we learn
to take things off,
to undress ourselves—
more disposed to meet,
almost naked,
the darkness and
the day.

I See by Your Outfit That You Are a Cowboy

Though I must have seen my father's face
in repose in some moments
when he was alive,
I'm not at all sure I remember them, and
now, if I were to come upon a photograph
of him not smiling,
I wonder how I would
recognize him, for
he went out every day to the world
that way, armed with assertive bonhomie,
humor that insisted,
an insinuating laugh.

He was needy—
not for wealth, or women, or liquor,
but, I think, for warmth. He grew up
not without a decent house
or things or money,

but nonetheless on the streets, eating at cafes
and hanging out at the gym,
or going to movies.
His father was kind
but stayed busy with work,
and his mother was cool,
curt, querulous,
her only laugh a staccato bark
corrosive with irony, and
she met any act of human kindness
by asking now why would they do that?
He and his brother were on their own.

He needed regular dinners around a table,
family talk and little league,
questions about his day at school,
and a familiar mantel
to hang a stocking in the holidays.

He gave me all that—
and nearly drove me crazy.

We were as different as father and son
could be, and I worked at it,
and I had a need to be left alone;
but as I advance in years
his impatience with sadness will
sometimes rise as a flush in my neck,
and I hear him quite distinctly in my
surprisingly corny jokes,
and feel his feet hurrying me over for
a hug with a friend, or find my brow
lifting to make a silly face at the sad child languishing
unregarded in the next line at the grocery store.

He hoped and I think he prayed
and so, I think, do I—when I dare to forget
my chill disapproval of my own hunger,
and let, as he did, daily billows of gratitude
carry us forward:
for we each found a good woman
who brought us in near the fire.

Sometimes I see us, just the two of us,

in a high unbounded desert,

and as the vast night presses us close,

the sharp commingled scent

of pinyon, dying embers, and the

feral, faintly sexual, tang of tarp

flays our senses open to the cold stars,

and he asks, without judgment,

looking out, beyond us, into blackness,

if I still have a chip on my shoulder,

and what's so hard about

actually taking the time to learn

to dive off the board correctly,

and I, looking just over his left shoulder,

ask him if he's still embarrassing himself

and everybody else by telling

for the ten thousandth time the one about

the poor lame man whose suit fits so well,

and thank him for sending me out to get

a good education and find Faulkner

and Kierkegaard and self-conscious anxiety,

and then we laugh, and make the bitter dregs

of joe swirl, and last in our tin cups

until it is time to go—

backward or forward

to where we belong.

Old Friends

Sometimes after getting together for dinner
or sometimes for no reason after a long passage of time
while pulling clothes from the dryer
or waiting at a red light
or brushing my teeth and glancing in the mirror

I see one of you
right there
in place of whatever is there

the angle of your chin in laughter
a certain sideways glance
some particular syllable of speech

right there
closer and sharper
than whatever is at hand

you are there
perhaps in your most recent incarnation

but often and every bit as vividly

on one of those days forty years ago
looking up across a table
or walking side by side in the mist
of a March afternoon.

We move on through time and place
called both to exotic adventures
and to be familiarly found
like the scent of daffodils
such richness never new
the scent of forever
always so surprising.

You Are

I'd like to say I've had the intrepid

and elegantly resilient mind

of one of those Renaissance guys

who learned how

to balance their days with dueling

and speaking fluent French and Italian

and discussing theology

and political science,

who also gardened and read philosophy

in the original Greek,

and then burnished their nights

with gracefully complicated dances

and writing passionate, inventively constructed

sonnets to their lovers,

and synthesized emotion and rationality

and irony without a second thought,

and happily imagined themselves

little lower than the angels.

But I can't say that.
I think that as far back into boyhood
as I can remember
I've always had an acquisitive,
grabby sort of mind,
afraid of everything I couldn't know.
The bottomless mysteries of life
did not strike me as beautiful,
or even acceptable—
they made me vertiginous
and kept me awake at night—
and even the facts so often seemed
dull, irrelevant,
or subject to change.
Humanism had paled.
And as for emotions—
well, let's just say I more often felt
like thick, rough strings, twanged
to little avail,
than a courtier with a dulcimer
and confident skill
sharing his soul in the moonlight.

But enough about me,
indeed.

And that's exactly what happened:
you.

You freed me from myself.
Perhaps I had to be that exhausted with me,
that impatient,
that dead-ended,
perhaps the readiness, indeed, was all.
All I know is that you came along
and coaxed the hostage out.

I found I could look into the night sky
and not feel completely hollow,
could go to sleep
without sensing the edge of the cliff,
could wake in something more
than disassembled fragments,
look out over the ocean
and not feel the world evaporating,

even look in a mirror and see

not a subject,

but a surprising object of love

to aspire to be.

I remember, a few years into our marriage,

coming out of the anesthetic after surgery,

and not just seeing you but somehow

knowing

what I was looking for, not seeing

only the expected cause of my gratitude—

the familiar, an anchor, a context—

but you.

I saw you—

the joy,

the reason,

the heart,

the hope.

O brave new world.

After decades

by tempests tossed,

I found

one inexplicable, unanswerable question

that did not disconcert,

and the only undeniable truth

that was needed:

the mystery of our love,

the fact of

your being.

New Year's Eve

Anyone who says they cannot understand
what manic depression must be like,
that it seems a state so alien, so beyond their grasp,
like Belarusse or Bhutan,
is not thinking clearly.

When the last left-overs
have been warmed over and are gone,
the last treats emptied from their tins,
the favorite music, that had been played
with inexhaustible elation, put away,

and the day began by standing
in the kitchen eating cold peanut butter on a cold oat bar
with large crumbs, whole chunks really,
falling maddeningly into the sink,
and now the hours slink along
like gray-brown scars
toward a so-called celebration,

each year earlier and more perfunctory,
you remember, so close, the open wounds.

Later this afternoon you will face coiling
the strand of small lights that brought
such a glow to the mantel
into the old hat box, and as you lower the lid
you will see them like the eyes of dead birds.
You know that if you yourself died
within the next twelve months,
someone would eventually open this box
and, even looking into those eyes,
would know very little about it all,
much less those marks, put nowhere at all
except in the sand you felt seeping,
those resolutions.

Trying to Nap

Some things never change.
I won the box of animal crackers
for being Most Still in kindergarten naptime
only once.
I don't remember the particular day. Perhaps I was ill,
or perhaps at recess the others
had all been mistakenly jazzed with Coca-Cola
rather than the regulation grape juice,
or perhaps Miss Dorothy wasn't quite
so complete a tyrant as I'd always thought
and had found some small soft democratic spot
in her Eisenhower heart
for a generally good, if wiggly, boy
who really tried.

As I lie now, decades later, on this
warm June afternoon,
a bit underslept as is too often the case,

utterly comfortable, so very willing,
the cat snoozing illustratively beside me,

I see that five-year-old clearly on the
insides of my eyelids,
my eyelids squeezed, like his,
like the tensile wings of butterflies,
and I am all too aware, like him,
of straining toward tranquility.

I count backwards from two hundred,
twice, then scrupulously wipe
a few persistent anxious files
of mental disc space.
I let the lullaby murmur of the ceiling fan
seduce me, gently lift me—
and I feel myself skim the surface of sleep
so serenely, so closely, that it is
like a cozying second skin, or one of the
water lilies we saw just this morning
still dreaming, heedlessly drifting,
extravagantly slug-a-bed,

down upon the pond.
I find myself thinking I might be
the hawk I saw yesterday casting off
as effortlessly as you please

from the top of a sycamore,
as one with a slow thermal,
a perfect parabolic curve, so high above
the field and back again, unmissed
by any watchful panting self;

or someone who had actually managed
to stay with those lessons in meditation,
now letting the material and the physical fall away
like gently drifting autumn leaves.

My consciousness lazily stretches out,
like my legs—uncoerced.

But now I feel a tickle in my nose
as the sun drops west
and one thin sharp shard of light

finds its way through the wooden blinds,

or I am betrayed by some infinitesimal flinch
of sinew or muscle, or some other bit
of the wondrous mysterious works that hold it all together—

perhaps some enzyme conducting
adroit negotiations with
the Greek salad we had for lunch—

or I am ambushed by one stealthy synapse firing
along a hairpin turn on the
non-chronological road of memory,

and there,
there is that boy again,
that boy who would always
find it so very hard to stop—
apparently afraid
that he might miss something.

Return Trip

When you spoke in your sleep
I looked over your shoulder
and the red digits showed 1:30 a.m.
Here, you had said—softly but quite distinctly,
as though in conversation, and evidently driving—
This is the road to my grandparents' house...There they are!

Now, hours later over coffee
in the gentle light of the porch,
you say you have no recollection
of this encounter with these people you last saw
alive and together nearly forty years ago
—but I'm happy you had me along, this once, to meet them.

Perhaps it is early morning, and perhaps
they too are seated on a screened porch—waiting for us—
crosswords in their laps.

Good country people, they probably are not enjoying

the scent of cinnamon in their coffee,

but for all we know it may be precisely

this moment of early September when the sun

inches over the next branch south in the buckeye tree

and the world is fresh.

That Boy from the '50s

I've seen him sitting at a small table
in that rose and aqua kitchen
at the row of windows farthest from the stove
coloring in his Peter Pan book while his mother cooks
and hums along with Patti Page or The McGuire Sisters.

Sometimes he's falling asleep in his room
as if on a boat rocking gently
on the ebb and flow of his parents' bridge club,
an exotic burnished horizon
beneath the door down the long dark hall
from which floats the odd oracular word—
Ike, Adlai, Hitchcock, Khrushchev—
on magic waves of muted laughter,
clucks and murmurs, Chesterfields,
Folgers, and White Shoulders.

And I want to reach down for this boy
and scoop him up and carry him away
before he's seduced by the era's mounting desperation

for conformity, for keeping up with the Joneses,
for winning friends and influencing people,
and by its fears—of Communism
and The Bomb, Desegregation, Outer Space.

But where in the world would I presume to take him,
in this world that's burning beyond anything
we could ever have imagined?

He's only recently appeared with such clarity,
usually when I wake in the middle of the night.
Unbidden by any dream or song cue
this child appears—you appear—
across the decades, just as clearly as can be.
What a surprise and how grateful I am.
If I'd known, I'd have run to the store
and looked for Baby Ruths
or some of those Sky Blue Popsicles you like.

I like seeing you in that time and place
of such insistent harmony
between the storms, that world which

the McGuires and Patti and Doris and Rosie sang sincerely,

with its coins in the fountain seeking happiness,

and the moon hitting our eyes like big pizza pies,

and even when someone was sad it was

a beautiful sort of sadness

about remembering a night

and a waltz in Tennessee—

so many pretty ladies hoping

that we may always be a dreamer

and may our wildest dreams come true.

I wouldn't dream of telling you

you haven't turned out

quite as I might have hoped—

and somehow I believe

you'll return the favor.

Seeing you so clearly now

gives me the chance to tell you

it wasn't your fault

that you lost innocence along the way.

It's not something we misplace

like our Davy Crockett cap

or the left ear for Mr. Potato Head—
it gets nibbled away,
and not by the Godzillas and the Gorgos

but by the everyday monsters of the world.
We seem now to have learned so much,
but to what avail?

Here, take my hand,
and—as Patti admonished—
we'll leave our fickle past behind us
and cross over that bridge.

I can't thank you enough for looking me up.
We can't relearn the innocence,
but I appreciate your coming back to remind me—
now, when it seems especially useful—
that when we do not know any better
there is nothing to fear.

So, let's always be a dreamer
and may our wildest dreams come true.

Acting at the Ice Cream Parlor

In mid-afternoon there are no other people about,

and he sits as anyone might on a hot day

at one of the three or four tables, each shaded by its big umbrella,

alongside the homemade ice cream parlor.

At first I think he is reading a magazine,

but as I walk toward the door

and pass within a few feet I see

that it is a crumpled flyer or newspaper insert.

It is upside down, and he bobs his head in animation—

looking down at the ragged pages and then up, back and forth—

and mouths unvoiced words with vigorous expression,

as though perhaps someone sits across from him.

If this were another story

the narrator would stop at the table on his way in

(perhaps recalling Fitzgerald's line in *The Last Tycoon*,

There are no second acts in American lives)

and, with tremendously casual off-handedness,

hold out a couple of dollars and say,

Will you let me buy you an ice-cream cone?

...It's pretty warm out here,

not staying, not even lingering, just a quick passing offer,

a small thing, something cool to accompany one's reading.

Instead, when I leave a few minutes later,

he has just risen and is beginning to walk

in sandals patched with duct tape.

Our paths cross diagonally,

and there is the briefest, very civil, exchange of glances.

In the unforgiving glare of the sun one of us

—lines forgotten, out of character—scuttles toward a car,

the other strides down the street, a spring in his step,

pages furled neatly under one arm like a jaunty broker's *Journal*—

face open with a daring smile.

Meeting the New Trees

Late in the afternoon

a week before Christmas

we wandered

through our end of the park,

reading the nursery labels

on the newly planted trees—

oaks of several sorts,

beeches, cypress, lindens for the bees.

When we left them standing

so straight in the snow

and headed home for a fire and a drink,

we strode lightly,

with singleness of heart

through the darkening blue,

filled with hope

sensing what we will never see,

our own blind youth reborn.

Screens

When the last light has seeped from the screened porch
and the trees begin to silhouette themselves
against the slice of peach that is the moon
we too assume a somewhat transformed mien

as now and then for moments at a time
we gaze into devices in our palms,
our faces glowing like the augurs of old
who bade signs and tidings from the air.
And when we then abjure this rough magic's
addictive mesmerizing lure and settle back
into our chairs and sigh and sip our drinks

and deeply breathe the laden beauties of
the summer night enfolding us we become
the generations who have for years before us
sat beneath such gently churring fans,
and in low tones we speak with idleness
of this or that and then for moments at a time

join in a perfect silent intimacy,

as cicadas and and crickets sing all around

and fireflies dancing just off the porch and

farther out among the trees gone indigo

make magic with no beginning and no end.

Mourning Doves

Even when some sudden sound or movement
prompts you to take to the air, you eye
the nearest branch with a hint of
resignation, as in, Here we go again—
a fox, a cat, that survival of
of the fittest thing—almost peevishly,
a flustered lumbering, a heavy ungainly
lift, hooting one repeating muted note
at the arduous inconvenience of it all.

You come around at the cocktail hour
and have become a fond familiar sight,
the two of you. I like to watch you strolling
in the dusk and hear you trail your mellow mezzos
through the grass, not quick or clever like
the finches at the feeder or so unbound
as the swallows to the mundane matters of the earth below,
but somehow quite companionable,
waddling there only a few feet from the house.
Even when disgruntled you have a sort of equanimity,

unlike the fractious jays and carping crows.

Neither giddy nor reactionary,

you eschew drama,

you do what you have to do

quietly and without hurry.

You seem to consider,

to take the measure of things.

To anthropomorphize is lazy and

presumptuous—but as I look at you

pecking the ground at the edge of the woods,

and you turn and look at me,

I imagine one of you saying to the other,

Okay, those folks up there on the porch

have got the right idea, let's knock off here—

my feet hurt and I'm ready

for a nice sit-down, a long cool drink, and dinner.

Later, as the moon begins to climb

we'll hear you croon the day to rest.

Your three descending notes

philosophically inquire—

without irony or angst or any hope of an answer—

who who who can know

the bittersweetness of the world

yet be, on the whole,

content.

Hush

My head has always been
so full of words
that I have learned to pay close attention
whenever I sense the absence of them,
whenever I suddenly become aware that a rare hush
has perched inside me
and is gently spreading its immaculate white wings,
and settling its plump round cooing bosom
into that hollow where the words
have ceased, for a moment, to swarm.

It is the wonder of that absence, that hush—
not the cumulative force,
the weighing, the sorting or choice,
the delighting or portentous patterns,
the searching,
of all those words—
that defines,
as perhaps one snowflake might
come nearer to doing,

what you are to me:

The quiet thrill
of perfect peace,
of home
beyond explaining.

Reading Chekhov Again

In a letter only weeks before his death
Chekhov told a friend:
I wish you all the best and hope
you will be happy and have a less complicated view of life,
because life is probably a good deal simpler
than you make it out to be.
Does it truly deserve all the anguished meditation
we Russians waste on it? Nobody knows.

This from a man who spent his life peering
through a pince-nez, prodding gently
at every human nook and nuance,
and who, at forty-four, had been discreetly coughing
blood into a handkerchief for two decades.

Critics knew he was up to something
with his delicate obliquity,
but they couldn't seem to take him at his word:
that the plays were comedies.
I describe life, he said, simply.

He never lectured his audience,
he sought their collusion.
They loved the plays but they, too, were uneasy, confused,
spellbound there in the darkness of the Moscow Art Theatre—
yearning with and for these characters, so familiar, on the stage,
crying with and for them,
wanting them to be able to change,
smiling when they could not—
such vision, hope, and longing,
such small-mindedness and sloth—
whom to pity,
whom to condemn?

He loved writing and he loved Olga.
The day before he died he began to improvise for her a story
about guests at a fashionable watering-hole,
how each reacts to the sudden decampment of the chef.
And sitting there beside his bed, wiping the sweat from his forehead
so that it would not trickle down into his beard,
Olga, ripping apart with anguish,
could not help but laugh.

In his ongoing arguments—
even with director Stanislavsky—
about the production of the plays,
he kept insisting that they should
be played not as dramas but as comedies.
He knew it was pretty funny
that whenever he sought peace in the country he pined
for the bustle and talk of the city, and when letting
the Yalta sun warm his pale skin couldn't wait to hurry back
to brace his laboring lungs with the icy Moscow air.

You ask me what life is.
That's like asking what a carrot is.
A carrot is a carrot,
and there's nothing more to know.

Modesty seems most clearly
to account for his gracefully borne impatience.
He didn't discount the metaphysical
so much as the presumption and waste
of trying to manipulate it.
In his notebooks he observed that we only belittle God

by presuming to grasp Him with our meager intelligence.

The only thing that dies in a man
is what is subject to our five senses.
Everything that lies beyond those senses—
and is most likely immense, unimaginable, sublime—
continues to exist.

It was a dignified acceptance that there is
so very much to life itself,
not the least of which are the questions—
but it wasn't defeatism.
Just because a script is tragic
doesn't mean it can't be acted otherwise.
That *irony* has come to be the word
most frequently used in considerations of his work
would probably disappoint him—
another lazy indulgence.

He wrote like the doctor he was.
His course of treatment was simple and constant,
more suggested, gently, than prescribed:
Look. See.

If you are hungry

and you are given a carrot,

eat it.

Gingko

This afternoon I drove past
a big round thick gingko
on what had to be
its most perfect day of
yellowness,
its yellowness
roiling in the sun,
and it was so intense
I suspected as I looked
into my rearview mirror
it was all the laughter
all the gold
all the daffodils
distilled
all possible
joy
impossible to deny
just bursting
bursting
all at once.

In the Wild

Sitting this evening in our screened back-porch
this last week of June we cannot escape
apparently momentous events in the lives
of our red-shouldered hawks.

Their shrieking *Why? Why? Why?* over
and over and over again unsettles us
with a perceived edge of hysteria, though our next-door neighbor
tells us her that call to the local Raptor Society was reassuring.

It's something that may be expected in early summer—
a mother telling her fledgling what's what,
or perhaps a couple scouting for a new abode
or reasserting a territorial claim.

Our quiet urban neighborhood in this old river town
is hilly and treed and no stranger
to all sorts of birds, rabbits, and occasional deer
who graze through the gentle green ravines and hedgerows.

For the past five days, though, the hawks' exotic cries—
above the other birds and for long minutes at a time—
have charged the air like a wild and misted rainforest instead
of a gently upcurving street with Dutch Colonials and chocolate Labs.

So we hope our neighbor has it right—
that there is no distress, only the noisy business
of child-raising or relocation—
and we lift our drinks to them.

What kind of neighbors would we be to read
some free-floating existential angst into
their insistent capacity for transforming a few of our
Kentucky twilights into something like Costa Rica or Belize?

For My Wife on Our Fifth Anniversary

We are, I think, even happier now,
though this planet has grown even more fragile,
its treed skin further peeled and blistering, cracked
by the wars and greed of feeble men still drawing lines in the dust
(only giddier now that an endgame is imaginable),
and still dragging God through it.

We have made our nest despite all this, and more,
taking heart even in the darkness that lets the stars be known.
We have found constancy,
and we cherish the recognition of yearning:
that too-early warmish wind in spring, brave but lonely, even lost,
trying the door and then slipping
around the house, pressing a fist at this window, then that,
yearning to come in to the hearth;
or two sycamores stretching toward one another
in a vasty moon-drenched field;
or, perhaps, two mountains sharply defined, snug, on the horizon;
or, perhaps—even seeing past the metaphors themselves—
we're just out here on our own,

somehow, real.

Beyond the wars, asphalted landscapes, and autobiographical failings,

a dispirited era's desperate urge to sensation,

beyond the suns and worlds and galaxies colliding,

the weeping through the void

of all those falling songs and bursting sonnets—

it will be your eyes,

your hand in mine,

that will have revealed the universe,

your smile,

some eternal brief glance or gesture,

that opened the true nature of things.

A Peppermint

Four days before you died, you lay
on your side, pulled in, fetal.
You kept your eyes closed,
made yourself small, waiting—
unable yet to be away.

The skin of your forearm was brittle,
almost translucent, and the hand
that curled in toward your shoulder fluttered,
touching a tissue to the oxygen feed
in your nostrils over and over again.
The only thing that you asked of this world
I could not give you.

I'd like, you said, a peppermint—for my throat.
And I said, Mom, I know that would be nice,
but with you lying down, and with that cough,
I'm afraid you'll swallow it.

Yes, that's right, you said, that's right—
and I gave you, again, a sip of water
through a straw.
Every two or three minutes,
you asked again.

My grandmother, your mother,
for decades kept peppermints
in a cut-glass bowl on the sideboard.

Once long ago at the beach,
after swimming and sandcastles,
after shrimp and hushpuppies
and coleslaw and French fries,
I asked for a second serving of ice cream.

You said you were sorry
but that I'd make myself sick,
and your beautiful face—so young, I see now—

shadowed for an instant with some fleeting

sorrow I could not understand,

regret that the summer evening and paradise

could not go on and on and on and on,

even for me.

Honey Locusts in Chicago

They are like mothers.
They are already in place every morning before us,
their arms writhing up and around so quickly,
so unconsciously, that we might think
we scarcely caught a glimpse of the hair going into place.

They are there all through the day,
their life-blood a felt, unnoticed vigor,
absorbing noise, standing along the sides
of our self-important busyness,
our awkwardness,
and all those occasional destructive
tendencies,
looking on,
keeping their own counsel,
not letting on what they know,
what they must be thinking
or feel,
but ready with a smile.
a subtle admonitory lift of the spirits,

just for the noticing.

They are there throughout the night,
breathing beside us,
asleep without sleeping,
stroking away the fever,
the bad dream,
so serene, so without disturbance
as to be almost a virtual touch.

They are there all the time,
year in and year out,
bearing the careless insults
and the cool self-absorbed indifference
of so many many thankless children,
standing constant in their strips of earth
even when it falls away,
tolerating the humiliations of
natural expansiveness wedged into
unexpected concrete exigencies,
trying so hard to be as large as possible for us
even when such unimaginable circumstances insist

they be smaller, more cramped than they

could ever have known to be,

their freshness and their seniority alike

implacable

in the face of benign neglect

and intemperate fumes.

They wait so patiently,

beside the park benches,

and down the street,

with dignity, a silent eloquence,

that defiant refusal to give up on us—

such unwarranted grace,

such a beautiful hoping

that we will come to our senses.

Alchemy

Alone, I sense,

half-wakingly hear,

then see—

a cardinal

rearing up on the highest branch of the poplar,

his head lifted,

directly facing the rising February sun—

and I feel his song

delicately pierce

the bright brittle cold

over and over and over again,

shattering it,

splattering it—

a liquefaction

of unadulterated joy.

I wonder only briefly

if he noticed me at all

standing there,

so still, beneath,

or, after a minute, moving on.

Whether he did or not,
I have liked to think
I've known him all this day—
and won't forget—
some tincture of his instinct,
of his orison overheard, spilled
on my person, carried
in my blood,
my dose of humility,
a remembered taste
of greatness.

In Black and White

Sometimes I simply have a need for black and white films
and it's not a precious whim or retrogression—
it's a recognition, a hunger.
It has nothing to do with pining for unreality
or an escape from our human world.

If anything it's an escape *into* the human world,
a place the seventh franchise
of a cartoon action hero can't take me
or computer enhancement digitally fix—
it's a way of facing life.

Of course it's impossible for anyone whose
earliest movie memories include
those Technicolor spectacles of the '50s
not to have an appreciation of color in film.
When Gordon MacRae lopes into the frame on horseback singing
that the corn around him is as high as an elephant's eye
our disbelief doesn't have to be willingly suspended—we pop it
with wanton insouciance like a gum bubble,

and when Grace Kelley and Cary Grant tear
along The Corniche in that convertible we feel
her pink scarf streaming back from that swan neck
and far below The Mediterranean is a coruscation of teal.

Still, when you've watched Atticus Finch at work in that courtroom
you have no need of remembering the various tints
of small-town suits or shirtwaists, complexion or hair—
you've felt the tension and the seething creep of sweat,
and you never forget sticking to those wooden benches,
waiting for justice to break.

And once you're introduced to Edward G. Robinson as Rocco
in *Key Largo*, smoking that cigar in the bathtub,
you do not have to know the colors
of his henchman's tie as he stands at the door,
to know that it is garish—and you will always know
the uneasy cruelty of thugs when you see it and remember
that soap suds can be the slime of pure evil.

When in *The Best Years of Our Lives*
your breath catches along with hers as Myrna Loy

knows for a split second *before* she knows and turns

from that kitchen to see Fredric March at the end of that hall,

it's because an entire universe comprised of them and you,

and complete in itself, is catching its breath.

Color is seductive and color is life

and who would want a world devoid

of daffodils and undistracted by

the fathomless blue of October skies?

But at times we need recalibrating,

and black and white takes us somewhere

outside our kaleidoscopic slice of life,

this crowded hour on the rushing cusp

of which we live.

It takes us outside time,

to those places in which our life is largely made—

light and shadow—the architecture

of images stripped bare, a truer artifice,

the most eidetic reality, the stuff

of memory and of dreams.

It takes the quickened eye,

unfettered by pigment and hue, deeper,

its tonalities speak directly to our heart,

and once seen, these films cannot be unseen.

So, in that last scene of *Now, Voyager*, when Charlotte tells Jerry

not to ask for the moon when they have the stars,

we're not wondering about the shade of Davis's lipstick

or what color the drapes may be—

there is nothing but the final swell of Steiner's theme,

the two glowing cigarettes lit from one, their one small strip

of territory they must protect, that window opened to the night,

and their eyes fixed forever on one another.

Habitat

I might feel more confident in civilization if
there were more evidence that we were doing it right.

Alone in the car this too hot morning in May
I happened to catch a few minutes of one of the Saturday
shows on public radio and it brought me up short.

A naturalist interviewed by the host
played a recording he'd made of wolves
in the wilds of Ontario.

I've never heard the like.

First one or two among the more usual sounds
of birds and insects and rustling wind and then
a massive haunted fugue gorgeous and raw
swelling up in counterpoint with something lost
an aching sharp enough to rive the night.

What will I do?

A bit more anguish, more advocacy, more awe

for the voice of divinity that managed to penetrate
the callous layers of compounding error
to find me here this morning.

Tomorrow perhaps more thought will follow
but for now I have the forest for a head
and darkness in my throat as I fly north
against the jet-stream knowing only that
I'll never be the same.

December Calibration

When we first look out
after the snow finally sifts
to its end in the afternoon,
we are stunned.
The clouds have not yet
parted and the early dusk
is already stealing up the hill
through the woods,
and we stand there, looking,
and can scarcely breathe.
Everything seems suspended,
everything has come
to a full and silent stop.

It is so opposite to the busyness
of the heavy storm crowding, constant
and engulfing, around the lights
of the porch last night,
and charging the air of the day with
such frenetically pure and delicate chaos

that we had to go trudging through it,

and even when back inside kept moving

from window to window to watch.

But now, in this first gray stillness

before the clearing and the night

and the icy staring stars,

there is this hour, this lull:

what sheer wonder,

like waking after a long,

uninterrupted sleep,

completely blank in the morning.

There, far along beyond

the curve in the road,

is the neighbor's house,

and, here, off to the left,

our small outbuildings,

and everywhere, the trees—

reconfigured in designs

much bolder than we remembered,

some straight, some bending,

some singled out as never before,

others crossing, in proud

and elegant embraces

kept secret in summer—

these silhouettes,

so black, so fresh,

so deep, so stark,

and this beautiful,

this exquisite snow.

It's all the same

but simplified,

a gorgeous abstraction

mesmerizing the eye,

and for a little while,

or longer if we're lucky,

problems and complexities

feel stripped to the bone,

a sharp clean slate

that something in us

like a child's hand

reaches out for,

an insistence

on starting over.

The Rate of Disappearance

Reading a magazine excerpt this morning,
from a new study published not by some crackpot theorist
but by a prestigious scientific journal,
I learn that New York, Boston,
Miami, and Holland are certainly doomed.

Since we are not taking our role in global warming
seriously enough, the oceans are likely to rise
nine inches within sixty years,
more than a foot within a hundred,
and before the next two thousand years
of what we have come to call The Common Era
have elapsed we're looking at eight feet.

The new, more frequent, more violent hurricanes are one thing,
but it's hard to imagine that any system of walls,
landfills, or pumps can hold back an entire ocean, and so

I wonder if some freshman class on one of Harvard's higher hills
may survey the broad estuary the Charles has become and laugh

that they, at least, have dodged the bullet;

or whether a father can explain to his child horizonless color
from the desiccated remains of tulip bulbs
they find stuck to the rafters of a ruined barn;

or if perhaps lovers on houseboats will be listening
in the fetid twilight to some vestigial rumba or merengue
as they drift over what used to be South Beach;

or if mothers pushing strollers on the Brooklyn Heights Promenade
may look west to a shriveling Manhattan and make some silent peace
with the rate of disappearance.

I can see myself at their age, careening along
in a subway, scarcely looking at the book in my lap
but re-seeing a scene in a play or a face across a bar,
or turning a corner on the Upper West Side
smack into a bitter midnight wind,
bending toward some future.

I watch until

the tunnels and canyons fill

with an alien liquid gray,

and then I turn the page.

The Last Snow

She asks to go out on the screened porch
for a few minutes where she sits silhouetted
against the whitened ground, licking her paws
and back-brushing her head, luxuriating
in the only kind of winter in which she sees
any point whatever. She knows it's an
unexpected evanescence, a gentle safe
amusement, and on her mouth and in her fur
she savors, secure from her prospect,
the vestiges of a good breakfast.

The snow keeps tumbling insistently down
yet even though the morning light is muted, ashy,
and obscured it still is nonetheless
the light of March, and the bright bare unthreatened trees
merely feign a ghostliness, murmuring
together, sharing the joke of their costume.
Like the cat on the porch they know
this is nothing to be taken seriously,

there is no ice, no bitterness, and in

a day or two the memory of this elegant

anachronism will tickle up their roots,

and the breeze, soughing once more from the south,

will tease goldfinches from their inmost branches,

congratulate the brave forsythia

and the flagrant youth of green and tender mosses,

and lift the waiting eager chins of daffodils.

Chere Madame
(for Estelle Carron, 1961-2012)

There is a lack of resolution here,

more than what we already knew of life,

with its way of leaving off and picking up,

its appalling stops and fitful starts all caught

together with rough and vivid seams and wild

ravelings of surprise and déjà vu.

We find ourselves with even more than our usual

baffled yearning, yearning from this sudden

gap, this gap between what was and is.

You are so much more here than you have known,

than your unassuming modesty would let

you see. Like most of us you are an improbable

mass of contradictions but you bear

it with uncanny grace—sophistication

innocent of hardness, the shrewdness of

an open child, a kindness that astonishes

those of us for whom such things come far

too slowly and infrequently, an elegance

not vain but of the fiber of a being

generous and gentle, an artless smile

utterly free of irony and freely given

to nurture and warm, no sentimentality

or cant, but joy and strength and fortitude—

sel de la terre.

Once again we learn how much we do not know,

how much a good woman and sweet soul

who gives and gives and never thinks to cast

a shadow is, we find, a teacher to

us all and, for once, admonishes us to try,

to take the time and care, to live more fully

for others and ourselves, to reach out

and reach for, or else we will be

oddly disunited not only each

from each but from her and our own selves.

Chere madame, you tell us that in France

they say that when you eat good bread you taste

the sun in the grain, so now we must always search

for the good plain bread that keeps the dark at bay

and fills us from this moment to the next
with the only certain thing we know:

that time and science cannot show
what brings us here or pulls asunder
the mysteries that seed and grow
such ravenous response and wonder,
and when we fall up through the stars
and this uncounted hour is gone,
nothing will remain but love,
only what is shared lives on.

Full Moon in Memphis

This bed is big enough for my comfort,
but it is too big without you.
Like Huck on his raft,
I drift between moon and dark water.

Any Horizon

When I realize that several days
have gone by without my looking at one
or at some congregation of them,
I am diminished—
but that doesn't happen often
for once I began really seeing them
about twenty years ago
I could no longer not see them.

Today it was a sycamore,
like a pale dancer, tall and proudly naked,
poised to stroke the distracted winter clouds,
and perhaps next week I'll be reminded again
that looking for the infinite shapes of cedars
maintains sanity on long unmemorable drives.
Later today, before the early evening, I may stand
for a moment in this rising wind
among the rattling tender reeds
of the willow behind the house

and let their cold dry rain clean my mind.

I know that the faintest line of lace-barked elms
redeems the grittiest city street,
a pair of flagrant maples can renew the eye,
and the right oak at any given moment
summon spirit.
I have learned so little,
but I have learned to reverence
the rest I find in your love—
this passionate peace—and I have learned
to reverence the trees.

You and the trees
are everything I understand of poetry
and everything I'll never understand,
I am alive with knowing you are
too much to comprehend,
you and the trees,
you stand for something—
the mysteries,
the boldest fact.

When I have no sense
of where I'm going,
I look again.

On any horizon I see
the trees and I see you,
and this is where I'm going.

The Ocean Spray Bushes
on Orcas Island

That you are ever called *common* says more,

and sadly so, about our human capacities than your own—

like some neighbor who ceases to listen

through the open window on an early summer evening

to that Mozart boy across the street

working out yet another tune.

In your brief brilliant season each May and June

you surge along the islands' roadsides—

arching on your frilly green branches,

catching the soft sun,

draping it against the rustling skirts of dark cedars

newly hemmed in emerald,

with frothy bursts of pendant geometries;

your creperie of white and ivory and cream

the most elegant show of all

on the long Midsummer's Eve,

perhaps even for the moon.

And then, in mid-July you begin—

with an impeccable sense of
taste, discretion, time, or breeding—
to fold yourself away:
yellowing lace, brittle and exquisite.

Common?
Whitman would have something to say about that—
well, the connotation of tone, anyway—
something like: *How about democratic,*
or generous, or even profligate?

Who are we so rich in eye and spirit
that we are not honored and enamored
to discover you dancing again this year
along the deepening shade of meadow rims,
the last phosphorescence of the twilights;
cascading cool at noon down rills and saddles;
or, all those mornings,
your choirs banked, so clean, nodding
along the open roads,
cheering us on.

Maerose

From time to time,
we gently mocked,
berating you for your finickiness—
your touch-me-notness,
the appalled and baleful glance,
the unhurried, disdainful, dismissive flick
of that preternaturally long, long tail.

But all the while, of course, we adored you for it.
Hauteur has rarely been so lovely, so winning.

Through household changes,
the nonsensical jealousies of siblings,
second-class travel accommodations,
through even your final illness,
you put down each paw with exacting elegance
and picked your own path through life.

You will always have the pinkest nose in catdom—
and, oh, those Cleopatra eyes.

Memorial

Today we drove through the summer green hills
to our favorite café and the shops in the next county seat
and, as usual, in this still rich ecosystem of the eastern mountains,
we drove through many, many insects.
Among them, in my own sort of odd Darwinian accounting,
it was only the four or five butterflies whose deaths I noted, and felt.

Somewhere along the way you asked,
And where are you now,
and as always at such times
I was embarrassed.

Not embarrassed in the way one can be
about moral ignorance and political stupidity and religious hatred—
no, none of that today—
but embarrassed for you to have caught me out
yet again in my distractions.

I am, thank God, with you
and drawing breath in this sweet, singular moment,

hurtling through this rain-cleaned world
of green and gold and blue.

Later in the afternoon, on the way back,
the worst of the lot: four inches wide,
sublimely black and yellow, coral and cerulean,
it lingered, mangled, shredding, at fifty miles per hour,
between the hood and wiper.

Oh, you said, and we both sighed.

Somehow—at least I tell myself—it's different
on the interstate, at seventy-five,
as though they should somehow know better,
or perhaps the splatting smears and tocking crunch
are only the smaller, less interesting innocents,
or even the bloodsucking bearers of disease.

But on this backwoods country road
arched with heavy woods and winding discreetly through
the soft deep-bosomed mountains whose cousins
not so far to the north are, unimaginably, still being topped,

there's time to wonder

how much longer we'll have

to keep redefining

collateral damage.

Most have a life expectancy of only weeks,

some merely days—the butterflies—

living only to commune with the flowers,

and to propagate their exquisite, gentle glamour.

They don't deserve to die like this.

But we drove on, and you

gave me a few more sidelong glances,

undoubtedly noticing, as you always do,

in the balance between

our effortless comfortable talk

and my furrowed brow

the confusion of those

with so much to answer for

being somehow happy,

like a forensics consultant

clucking over evidence,

sifting and swabbing for explanations

of life as we now know it,

or perhaps a rather prim janitor

who loves his work,

or at least finds it hypnotic,

discovered after hours,

obsessively trying to sweep

into ever straighter lines

the incessant carnage of beauty.

October Clean

The fog in the gorges and hollows at first light
is like cold remembered rivers mapped in sleep,
still dreaming, languid, silver, long and deep—
for minutes then it's sun-shot snowy white;

so in October the seasons converge from hour to hour—
self-effacing, old, accustomed friends,
asserting, yielding, no grudges, no bitter ends;
this openhanded grace accrues a power

that eclipses January's touch of death,
the manic flights of March, its anguished falls,
seductive April's giddy, fecund calls,
and August's clotted, immolating breath;

and through the sycamore and hemlock steal
at noon the wood smoke's evanescent traces;
each eidetic oak and maple in ardor faces
the other, harmonizing, and we feel

them pulling us out of doors, wiping the mold

of any memory not vital or forgiving

and any melodrama not worth living

as something cleaner—sharper—blue and gold.

In Transit

Since morning, scattered flights of snow
have scudded through the air as if they had
been sent without directions or intent,
without sufficient numbers to fill
the atmosphere or turn the landscape white.

And lingering at windows I watch them pass,
as, missionless, they push on as they may,
not like the teeming millions of a storm,
but solitary, brief, and singular,
undestined, misbegotten, and misspent,
—yet with their own distracted dignity—
through grayness undefined as this or that.

The Air is Charged

We cannot know if there is more behind
than lies ahead, but the air is charged as ever
with that endless eagerness for what
comes next—color, frost, snow, silhouettes.

We know these seasons pass and we must go,
but these realities that we have known—
the kindness shown when nothing else would do,
the cruelty, the war, the pain, the loss,
the breath of leaves when rain has slaked the drought,
the longing beauty twilight thrushes tell,
and learning , most of all, that love is real—
who or what could have imagined all of this?

The world was not created long ago
once and for all but is created every
day, and if we find that love is the greatest
thing our need has made us dream—as real

as passing seasons, mountains, seas, and stars—

then call it dream, or need, imagining

or faith, or spirit, God, or what you will.

Somehow we knew that it was real when we

found it or it found us, and far beyond

our transient dust this dream of what is real,

this reality of dreaming lives. That such

a thing can be imagined may indeed

be all we have, but whether there is some

other great awakening, long sleep,

or nothingness—whatever worlds collide

or fade, this cannot be denied:

we love.

He and Alice Adams Go Way Back

Late on an evening in June a man—shaggily attractive,
older but not yet a truly old man—lies propped
in bed, the book in his hand illuminated
by a reading lamp. He loses his place
again and again as he runs the tips of his fingers
along the wavy edges of the pages
of a book of short stories (by a master
of the form) he has not read in nearly thirty years.

The stories and he have not parted ways—
if anything their exchange is even richer,
deeper, more generously kind than before—
but it is the book itself, the slightly bowed hardback,
these rolling-edged pages that keep taking his eyes
from her words, his own elliptical narrative
that distracts him.

The publication date of the collection
(he's read them all) provides a rough timeframe—
within a chapter or two of his life—

but as the rain and thunder of the summer night

roam around the dormers, he wonders

where precisely was this book that the edges

of its pages now softly undulate like this?

Where did he take a favorite author

for company at this particular time?

Some North Shore beach on Kaua'i?

A hotel spa or steamroom in Denver

or possibly Atlanta? A friend or second cousin's pool

from that era? And why?

The date is a few years before

his mid-life marriage which, nearing twenty years,

has been beautifully—astonishingly!—happy.

Was it a break from professional busyness

or some ill-conceived affair,

or was it held tightly in the wake of the last round

of that sporadic relationship which, like some creature

from a horror film, too long refused to die?

Was it read for the sake of pleasure,

comfort, art, or to dull pain, to heal?

He wanders through that time searching
for specifics—here, there, each remembered
action, setting, piece of dialogue leading
to others. Few are definitely fixed
and even fewer clear.

He settles his back, adjusts the reading lamp,
as the rain gentles into a murmur
on the windows and the roof, and he
alternately reads and travels in time.
He meets the stories with a sense of shape, shadow, tone,
and that rich familiar fondness that drew him back—
but their voices, faces, bitterness,
sophistication (real and imagined),
humor, surprise, loss, and he
have been just long enough apart
to bring new discovery, revelation.

Beside him, beyond the pale circle of light,
his wife (already asleep) stirs slightly
and peaceably inhales, and he lets the book
lie on his lap, and there are no other thoughts

or images as, for a moment, he watches her there
and hears only the soft rain as
the world turns wonderfully on through space.

Soon he will switch off the lamp and close his eyes,
listening to the rain and feeling other nights
and days and decades passing one another—
like old friends shouldering companionably
through a gathering to take turns
on a terrace looking out across now darkened water
toward the evening lights just coming on
in some lovely, distant view—
as he wonders (with both nostalgia and curiosity
but with really very little unease or worry)
how it all turns out.

September

Like adolescent boys bewildered
by their late summer growth spurt
gangly Joe Pye some over six feet tall
blush dusky mauve heavy-headed
and nod vaguely toward the ground
and the sturdy Queen Anne's Lace of June
now vestigial kneels to fold itself away
but all around the roiling ochre
of black-eyed susans and goldenrod
the purple ironweed and carmine sumac
exult like clever children in their
last burst of guttering glory just before bed
their insistent fey ecstatic shrieks echoing
all the witness they can bear
to the blue blue sky and even bluer hills.

The Old Oak on Route 27

I didn't really see a tree
until I was nearly fifty or if I did
I was unaware of doing so.
Now I see them
everywhere
like a blind man healed,
always marking my days
always in my sleep
forever swaying
the clear water of dreams.

One I have come to count on
is on a country road.
Our house is only twenty miles to go
when it appears in isolated splendor
against a wide open field, alone
one assumes for decades, long before I
became an admirer.
It's one of those oaks so strong
and simple and magnificent

that it always strikes
like one of the few incontrovertible
truths of this life.

It appears—when we
have been a longer time away—
more, not less, there,
even though it is growing old
and thinning at the crown,
branch by branch
yielding to the sky—
sometimes a limb here or there
at its feet.

I wonder if one day
we will find it
split or fallen.
Will it go first,
or I?

It is so there for me,
for anyone who has passed

and had the urge
to see,

whether sheltering
a few cows on August days,
or its bare-knuckled roots clinging
harder every winter
the wet eroding embankment.

It is so there
it cannot not be.

If one day
it is no longer there
I will long for it,
yet I will always see it as it was,
as the world was then;
and that cannot be
merely a matter
of synapses,
rods, cones,
photoreceptors,

but of something as well
that steals relentless through the soil
of rotting leaves, the veins,
the endlessly convulsing air,

refracts, explodes, assembles—
impulse, laws of physics, God,
some kind of love and hunger.
I wonder but do not care.

There it is,
where it was,
here.

In the Bargain

She says she was a little surprised
when he asked her to marry him
thinking perhaps that cohabitation
might be the likely next phase of
their relationship.

He did it because he wanted to give
her everything—
the recognition
or acceptance
or beginning
or embracing
of a world—
and he himself was effectively
all he had to give.
There was no wealth to speak of
some modest talents
a not indecent character
a not unattractive appearance
flaws

humor.

So in the most essential way

(and he likes to think it may please her

to think of it so) he gave himself

in marriage—*was given in marriage*—

not wholly unlike women in many societies

had been for era after era

not the sort with dowry or expectations

but in that other basic way of barter

as a mate, a partner,

for life's unfolding.

It was not parents who did

this thinking, this arranging,

nor was it social mediation

or circumstance.

The only broker was a uniquely forged directive of

imagination, necessity, faith.

This is yours

is what he was saying—

to use as you may

cherish as you will

discover further as you go along.

Though filled with sentiment about

the thing itself

the fact of love

he approached the asking

without undue sentiment

a stunning lack of hesitation

clear-eyed:

he had an ache of need

and he had a modest hope

of being of some help.

He knew this: it was

a complete, a total, passion.

He wanted the absolute

the irrevocable

he wanted to risk everything

to tell God and all

with humility and pride,

Take this fate and seal it.

Now years have passed

the passion has billowed
and steeped—
his love sees no bottom
no end

yet his need has been reduced
to a daily dose of belief
that by letting him give all he had
true and whole
whatever it is not
she too has sealed a fate
with something
reassuring, useful,
good, or great,
forever
in the bargain.

Stay Warm

In the end it was the heat vent behind the sofa,

no longer my lap or the crook of my arm late at night.

You've always known where to be and what to do,

beginning with your insistence

at our front door all those years ago.

You'd had enough of that hard life on the street and lay

so that for three days we could not avoid you,

had to step over you, had to see your molting fur,

your wasting away.

You've always known

where to be and what to do.

We grew so fond

and you grew beautiful.

It was a good move.

You chose us well,

and not a day since

has been wasted.

A Walk in Early October

The black and yellow bee

so fat still feasting slowly rides

the swollen goldenrod down

down and the garish green globe

of the bois d'arc thuds with heavy fatality

near a squirrel too busy to look up—

his frenetic wheelings from

burnished grass to oak

not unlike my grandmother

putting things up in jars

her kitchen frenzied

with what I assumed

were the mad movements

of an absent-minded old woman

but now can see were a ballet

grounded in instinct

mapped with precision.

Although there is a sunny warmth

it is thinner as if the atmosphere too ripe

has burst after the coldest morning so far

the birds at noon still rustle
in convocation in the trees and bushes
an accelerated velocity of speech
a tense merriment of tone
did you feel that? did you feel that?
considering new remembered plans.

All around
such watchfulness
such cheerful submission
things gathering in
tending down
bending down
going down
down to earth.

You are far away
but in a dream at dawn
on the freshest purest air
were close enough for me to pull

with the edges of sheet and cover
your arms onto my shoulders
and we walked as I do now

bearing our rich harvest lightly
smiling to the day
the frost made clear.

Tight Ship

Sometimes when I jot a note on a scrap of paper
to remember something I need to do
I will then take a pair of scissors
and trim the jagged edge of paper
to make it even, but I don't think that's alarming
in the grand scheme of things—and it's
only when the scissors happen to be handy.

I don't have to take six sips from the same side
of a glass and then switch, or regularly count lampposts
as Ben Franklin was rumored to do—and even if that is true,
he turned-out pretty well, didn't he? And I can make peace
with writing-over in a crossword puzzle even though it does introduce
a sense of irreparable compromise—as though you've found a flaw
in a shirt you like in a shop but take it home anyway.

Neatness may be as close to godliness as I ever get,
so I try to embrace it. If you want the throw pillows
on your sofa or chair adjusted with a certain *elan*, I'm your man.

Books stacked on a lamp table with a practical eye to size and shape

and an aesthetic consideration of color? You need not lift a finger.

Relationships labeled, decades filed.

With the edges of the cover folded in a crisp line

across my chest in bed at night, I alternately scrutinize

the manifest and stare at a borderless sea,

until finally I am lowered, with the only duffel bag I own,

into a ship I did not summon—I sense the lapping of the water, and then

sail off without a rudder through a disorder of uncharted years,

of images and feelings too rich and strange to sort.

Thaw

Walking down the street today
I stretched with the hemlocks and the pines
as they began to breathe and stir again,
and even made some sense of silly squirrels knocking
down chunks of loosened ice along the gutters,
and in the crowns of oaks cardinals blazed red
against the unfathomable blue sky and sang insistently,
and the whiteness glared and we
all exhaled together, breathing
down into the earth and up into the sun,
and now and again for moments at a time
my veins and footsteps and thoughts became
branches, roots, clouds,
and water running free.

Christmas, Again

When I was a boy, even though you loved the little children,
all the children of the world—red and yellow black and white
we were precious in your sight— as far as I could see
in my Sunday School only white children were singing.

And before that you were carried off
to slaughter infidels in The Crusades
and during The Inquisition invoked for torturing non-believers,
and the Victorian colonialists made you muscular, marching as to war,
their royal master, forward into battle,
leading against the foe, and seeing their banners go—
planting flags and plundering people and resources.

Where are you now?
For several decades an implied decree has gone throughout the land
that you have been hijacked yet again, sequestered
almost exclusively by one political party, your name used
yet again to let people whitewash fear and vitriol
and absolve them of critical thinking.

You must be really tired of it—even the best teachers
need to believe in at least occasional good results—yet
every year you come again to remind us of ideals.

Love our neighbor as ourselves, feed the hungry, take care of the sick
and the old, and allow children to know love.

And learn, over and over again, how to love,
and not to rant on the airwaves but go into our closets to pray,
not be easily provoked to anger—
much less accept hatred fed on your name
as a cruel wedge and bludgeon.

Oh lonely, misused Christ,
remind us once again to be patient and kind,
yet stand up when it matters,
to learn over and over—
and over and over and over again—
how to love.

I Would be White Tulips

You have many favorites throughout the year—
cerise cyclamen, hellebores, daffodils,
yellow roses, chrysanthemums—
but for your birthday it must be white tulips.

I don't remember your ever asking—
it's an unspoken rapture I've discerned
over the years like discovering
the atavistic keenness we share
for the great songs of the '40s,
which particular phrases from a handful of tunes
cause you suddenly to murmur along and sway,
something you rarely do, something
that reinforces the image of you
as the girl you are.

I would be white tulips,
perfect pale flesh rounding out of celadon
in a cut-glass vase on the small table,

gleaming in the early sun

for you to see first thing

when you come downstairs—

not newly cut and just brought home

but on that fourth or fifth morning,

when I am bowing toward you

as mated swans do,

yearning out with all I am,

to be at once with you

in the fullness of that grace,

the memory that always brings us home,

that brings now a little catch to your throat

as you turn at the foot of the banister and see me,

and *Heaven Can Wait* or *The More I See You*

shimmers golden-moted

in the morning light.

Dailiness

I've never prayed along a strand of beads
or bowed on a prayer rug five times a day,
but I may have heard echoes of Tibetan chants
or pilgrim steps across the hills of northern Spain
when I rub wax into the old table
and buff back and forth, back and forth,
look for shadows, then stroke it again
back and forth.

Raking leaves brings that stir
of reaching out again and again,
like a swimmer pulling through the clean October air,
the making of the mounded stacks,
here the wheelbarrow for the compost heap,
and there, along the walk, all those
brown recycle bags waiting pleated and tall.

I've even sensed I might be onto something
simply standing in the laundry room,
in the gray oblong of winter light

from the one small window,
and carefully shearing warm lint
like wool from the filter.

On an afternoon walk a few days ago
I saw an older couple walking from their car
up to their porch. He stood to one side
as she opened the door and they went in.
I don't know them but I do happen to know
that he recently had surgery
for stage-four brain cancer.
I can't see behind their door,
but I know their litany is changing,
and the eventual question we all must face
is whether ours will turn bitter or sustain.

As I go from room to room
turning on the lights at dusk
I know what I cherish,
the familiar pattern forged
by finding the button on this lamp cord,
this reaching once again for the switch

on the sconce above the stair.

When you come into the room
and we sit down with our drinks,
let's toast the sturdy wonder of having been
here yesterday, the day before,
always on the cusp of unknown waves
like birds migrating half the globe
because it's what they do.

We make our paths
and join the world
with these recognitions,
these rhythms,

this dailiness,
as improbable as everything else,
an impulse in the scheme of things
that somehow finds its place.

Late August

Maturity doesn't seem to help a bit,
in fact it makes it worse: again the end
of a summer gapes, a wound that will not mend
despite resolve, philosophy, and wit,
green days of lazy walks and schedulelessness,
long drinks on the porch and books and dinner at nine,
cicadas, tree toads, hemlock scent, moonvine,
the silly joke, the unexpected kiss.
So long as (I say, as I plead once more to reason),
the fabric of this being remains intact
I'll survive this month until you too are back
and not succumb to alarms and rush and noise,
draw evenly on the cool remembered joys,
sweet summer as our life and not one season.

Palliation

In the cool of the morning
I went out, underslept,
to treat my beautiful tree.
Hemlock woolly adelgid.
Adelges tsugae.
In a shallow trench around its base
I poured the highly toxic mix
but all the while I thought about you,
our last reports of you,
and poorly differentiated neuroendocrine *carcinoma*.

In the uncharted hours after midnight
the boat casts off again,
flimsy, cracked, unpurposed,
on tarry brine pleated back
by the sucking ebb of what we know,
glistened with the clinging slime
of all our ignorance and fear.
On some unseen shore the ghosts
of crumbling henges loom

in lurid torchlit shadows.

I hear druids, I hear chanteys rolling
rough like dark misshapen pearls
in the throats of sailors outward bound,
I hear the loving and the loveless
murmur incoherent hope and despair.
Blackness pulls beyond the pale
and I listen for someone known
to call to me.
I know nothing, but somehow,
somewhere, behind or beyond,
I seem to know the trees.

The national forestry people tell us
they are treating every day now
over in the mountains.
I cling to the effort
of saving those we can,
these few particulars.

We cannot save whole forests,

save our whole selves,

but we dig the shallow trench and

fill it with the toxic mix,

into deeper holes here and there,

foreign ports in yielding bodies.

A friend recently offered a definition

of prayer which seems to me as good as any

I know at defining the indefinable:

perhaps, she said, it is simply

the offering out of any small goodness

that we may have.

In this dreamy fatal illness that we share

we know good only as we learn to feel it

here among the poisons, persisting.

Whether, as an apostle says,

we are rooted and grounded in it, or only

kept awake by the unnamed yearning,

around you we have dug the trench.

You have us coursing through your veins

with everything we've got.

Encounter

Walking this late May afternoon
I pass, sitting very erect on a neighbor's lawn,
an old robin, breast pale, wings mottled, frowsy.
Its gaze, however, appears alert—
only a few feet away, unmoving, it stares at me.
I stop, and stare back.

It seems very old indeed.
I feel that. But though I do not presume to know for certain,
it seems all right, content, standing there,
standing straight, taking in the sun.

Can it no longer fly?
Will it hop in resignation
beneath the nearby hedge of cool clean laurels?

Is its instinct like our imagination?
What does it imagine—some faraway morning when it sang
one particular song that turned heads in all the trees around?
The easeful grace of flight from limb to earth and back again,

selfless, seamless, one with the evanescent

elemental dream of sublime chaotic order?

After some time I walk on, then turn to look at it—

its head turns just perceptibly.

We look once more at one another.

What does it see?

What do I salute?

Is it consciousness not circumstance

that makes the happy and the sad?

I go on my way, into the knotted shade of oaks,

leaving the bird standing there, still,

still basking in the sun—

awaiting,

not worrying,

what next.

With You

We didn't know it would be like this,
in this land we've come to,
beyond those middle decades so charged
with the hard-driving narrative
of I and you and it and them.

Who could have guessed
that we would find ourselves in a new
more knowing childhood,
looking, really looking, all eyes,
in wonder at the world,

at a gorgeous goldfinch just off the screened porch
that breakfasted with us, nibbling in studied nonchalance
as an unprepossessing nuthatch showed off
strutting up and down the birdfeeder pole eating sideways.

We were too preoccupied, of course,
in the earlier years of our stories
to detect the fine details or grander patterns

or any foreshadowing of our mortality,

rushed as we were by a ravening need to make it up as we went.

We unwaveringly loomed so large there was no space

left over for shadows—like that dark long-fingered hand

reaching now in the last light

from the buddleia toward the shed

through the tender blue grass.

It is some compensation to know we now

fit differently in time,

that when we wake to hear the thrushes' song

so insistently different from their vespers,

or stared after dinner last night in the table's candlelight

into the passionate bronze geometries

at the heart of a purple coneflower,

the life-and-deathness,

though even more urgent,

is somehow

so much broader,

deeper,

richer.

We will die by specifics,

that's clear from all the evidence,

but it becomes ever clearer, too,

that we live by them—

and something more.

It is even some comfort to know

how much less we know as we go,

making way for modesty

and mystery,

to feel it unfolding,

ourselves unfolding,

imagining, and choosing to believe,

that what we share, and how,

leads us to discover.

Following the Moon

As we watch the seasons pass
we try to believe in the rightness of letting go—
but what we always want is to keep.
Since you first showed me almost three decades ago
what happiness could really be,
it's become a restless ambition—

we want it always, for the rest of our lives, forever.
Despite believing that we will always be drawn by it
as the moon-track seems to draw a boat across the water
and that once we know, we *know*,
we keep having to remember that the hardest thing
is not to let such happiness make us sad.

Tonight as we linger on the porch,
delaying dinner and sipping our drinks,
I in the rocker and you in your swing,
I watch the plump full moon, a worldly boulevardier,
saunter up behind you through the old white oak,
his apricot complexion flushed with a wry smile and tipsy wit—

but then suddenly he rises, thinner, paler,
more innocent, more lithe and somehow younger,
his constant changes imperceptible
unless you've looked away for a second.
He quickens his pace upward, beyond time,
leaving his sophisticated past behind,

exchanging a personality that commands attention
for a presence that reveals—
and for a few moments as you give that little laugh
that's something between a syllable and a sigh,
gently frames your head with such a perfect halo
I feel I might reach out and touch it.

Waiting for October

Perhaps September is the time when our impatience is sent
to the emergency room and we are left in an anonymous waiting area
where we languish in the pallid light and over-breathed air
and become dry as bones, dry as the rattle of daydreaming leaves—
when dryness dulls the world except for a shared distracted fidget,
a twitch in the leg, a hawk's cry, a hedge-apple thudding in the dust,

as we wait—and even the harvest moon looks parched
and fixes a baleful gaze on the northwest, waiting—
as we all, as everything, waits—for the winds heavy with rain
to quicken the pulse and bring a flush of color,
moisten lungs and soothe the stiffened limbs.

It's an in-between time—summer's last passion expended
but weeks before defining clear-eyed frost—a restless suspension
when we are left to wonder what came before and what will come
and who and how and what and why we ever expected
whatever it was we thought would materialize in the way

of who we might have been or who they were or why

that particular something—that love or hate, idea, dream, question—
never came, or why it never went away, or why
we find ourselves still waiting to come to our senses,
ready for the wild wet winds to rise.

Still

Under a big black umbrella I head out

for a walk in the December rain,

down the lane through the woods.

The trees and brush are a seamless black and grey and brown,

held in place here and there by cedar, pine, or holly,

and there is no one, no movement,

and no sound except my feet moving below,

my breath if I choose to see it,

and the blank silver light

of the world turning gently in upon itself.

Only once I stop, surprised

by white feathered wands or magic plumes

bobbing up and down on the left—

four deer bolt away, stop and turn forty yards off,

and we regard one another.

While down the road and around the hill

you are at a neighbor's

for your afternoon of bridge.

This moment is a world

as I might dream it to be,

a clean new moment

yet perhaps somehow remembered.

I am entirely occupied,

absorbed, as if it were something

I am working on, but I am not:

no particular sense of self

no rattled cage of needs,

no elations ending as they begin,

no unfulfilled conditionals,

and not even a need to know

what it means.

The only turning in the road ahead

is the turning in the road ahead toward home,

and joy the invisible inward busyness

of the silent winter trees all around

and the assertive irregular hiss

of cold rain on clean crisp gravel.

Cardinals

This morning, while sitting in my usual chair
sipping coffee and manipulating my android
to check out the world
if not on my terms
at least with an illusion of control,
I looked up to see, through the french doors,
a congregation of cardinals on the deck.

There is no proper feeder out there,
and with all the squirrels there wouldn't be much point,
but there they were, twenty or more,
the males impossibly red, the females an elegant pistachio,
swooping about, sitting on the rail, trading places,
as though their entire *raison d'etre* was to flout
—be seen against—the gray, dank, January morning.

For several minutes their sheer numbers
kept the ubiquitous squirrels at bay,
and I had them, as it were, all to myself.
Or, rather, they had me. In fact, I was hardly there at all,

and if I had been of more significance,

or even been noticed through the paned glass doors,

the radiance would have fled.

In the Gutted Kitchen

The kitchen stands gutted down to the studs—
and before the drawings take on drywall muscle and flesh
and bring to life the vision of new mornings and evenings,
it's good to stand here for moments at a time
in the bare-ribbed quietly breathing past.

Over all the years your interests and mine converged
only here and there, but that never really mattered.
You could not have cared less about literature or trees or philosophy
and what I know about the more obscure members
of the latter-day Romanovs and porcelain and old silver
would fit into one of your Regency marrow spoons—
but I married your cousin and we became cousins
and that, as you often said, was that,
and much more than enough.

The new insulation there on that exterior wall
was desperately needed and is neatly done,
but we all know it will never be enough to muffle
our decades of reverberating laughter.

And though the library was the scene
of some of the more epic parties—
and you were the best kind of host,
your good form arising not merely from
an adherence to rigid form for its own sake
but from a thoughtful concern that everyone feel at ease—
I think I see you most clearly here, in the kitchen,
the kitchen with the prehistoric oven you would not replace
so that you could buy that Georgian satinwood card table
or another Faberge egg.

(One of the two bathrooms is also gutted
and the other is receiving a fluff job—
the mid-century fixtures and the cabinets stuffed
with fossilized products labelled 29 cents are gone—
but that is another story. I do not find myself standing in them,
looking and listening, waiting for
the heart of the house to beat again.)

This kitchen is liberated now
from the worst orange and green excesses of 1968—
here where we talked as you prepared dinners that invariably

included cream of mushroom soup here, a little Velveeta there,
as we sipped our scotch and occasionally tuned-in
to the one passion we did share—the old movies
emanating day and night from the small tv set
in one corner of the cupboards.

We do not plan on having one in our newly emerging kitchen,
but I suspect that from the corner of my eye for years to come
I will see a flicker of Myrna Loy, Gable or Hepburn, right there—
just over the drawer that went away
along with its fifty-year-old gadgetry
that didn't pass muster for Goodwill.

And we will lift a glass to you
and to the heart of things—
these places we share
that hold secrets, trust, eccentricities,
the best of times, love—
to spaces and relations
that never will be finished.

Seeing the Light

In the woods last night, away from the glare of the city,
we went out to stare at the silent rushing gush of Milky Way,
blazing cold and white and somehow remembered
as if it were in our blood.

We were small and silver blue beneath its grand self-absorption,
and tried to reconcile its cool-eyed luster with the fact
that it tugged at our guts and carried our eyes beyond themselves
and we felt ourselves reeling in some sober stillness.

When I mentioned having read that some early humans thought
this path of incandescence was a pilgrimage they already had begun,
you reached out and tugged my arm, then held my hand
as we walked back toward the house, the lights from the windows.

Labor Day

On a quick mission through Target yesterday

we slowed nearly to a stop as we passed

a section of aisles laden with back-to-school supplies...

Oh, oh...

...the notebooks with untried spines,

the pristine sets of virgin markers, pencils, pens,

notepads of all sizes for yet-to-discover words

and sentences of great import, and hieroglyphs, runes,

doodles, codes, and secrets,

and, most beautiful of all, enveloping us

in that waxy rich reassurance

of remembered beginnings and new adventures,

the color-chorused scent of crayons,

suspending us there for a moment

like young bees in flowers,

between borders brightly drawn

and blank space deep and rumored.

Afternoon Quartet

Waiting for friends to join us for a late lunch
I catch a glimpse through an archway
of one of the few still occupied tables—
four well-turned-out women,
all near ninety—and find myself
settling into the murmur of their soft voices.
An occasional word in the ebb and flow
is discernible, but it isn't what

they are saying that holds me,
it's how they say it—which isn't to say
that what they are saying isn't of note to them—
only that, sitting several feet away, it is
the slight modulations of the low volume,
of the tone, that mesmerize me.
Without presuming, it does indeed seem
that the *what* of it all has become

less important than the *how*, that the
shared concern and focus

is on making a song together.

Our friends arrive and we move on,
but I could sit there much longer,
knowing that it is my own advancing years
that allow me to hear the coo of an unsentimental
caress in this convocation of mourning doves,

this seasoned quartet of women—
partnering, supporting,
each doing her part for the whole,
for a beautiful music they are weaving.
Were I closer I might hear a name,
a date, a place, someone or some thing
remembered, or forgotten, but I'm convinced
that it is the sheer gathering

of the nearly four centuries that draws them on
beyond any individual need to stand out,
beyond knowingness,
gossip, irony, pronouncement—to a place
in which they are glad in some new harmonic way

to be at lunch in a good restaurant

on a fine summer day,

keeping this balloon in the air—

making this music together,

savoring an occasional pause

to look out to the river beyond,

where pleasure boats flash

past the windows, almost too quick to see,

and long barges nose their way upstream,

too generously laden to hurry but getting there

all the same.

Green

By the end of March the greening
of each succeeding day becomes
an imperceptible drama of difference—

an imperceptible greening of promise,
surprise breaking again from black skeletons and cold mud
and chasing away the last of winter
that has been at our heads like a mob of starlings.

I know that this morning the trees and hedgerows
were somehow far more lush than yesterday
and I watched for awhile
trying to catch them at it—

irrational as minutes go—
but far beyond value
and somehow beyond time,
like that those two consecutive time-lapsed moments

when I can see the returning of your love,

that half-smile that rises in your eyes

before you remember all there is to know of me

—everything—

and choose to say I love you

anyway.

HADLEY HURY's poetry has appeared in numerous journals, reviews, and magazines, and he is the author of a novel *The Edge of the Gulf* and a collection of stories *It's Not the Heat*. He was for many years film and theatre critic for *The Memphis Flyer*, has been a contributor on film to *Insider Louisville*, *The Lost Coast Review* in California, and *The Flaneur* in London, and was an associate professor in film studies at the University of Memphis. He has worked as a senior executive in non-profit organizations focused on the environment and women's and children's health, and was also chair of the Department of English at Hutchison School. Passionate about trees and urban reforestation, he has implemented and directed neighborhood tree-planting initiatives both in Louisville and in Memphis, where he now lives with his wife Marilyn Adams Hury.

Made in the USA
Columbia, SC
31 October 2020